THE FRUGAL MILLIONAIRE

Seven Money Management Principles to Help you to do More with Less

RAVI SODHI

Copyright © 2017 Ravi Sodhi

All rights reserved.

ISBN: 1542780357
ISBN-13: 978-1542780353

DEDICATION

To my wife Pinky whose unconditional love and devotion help me overcome all kinds of negatives and allowed me to complete this book. And to my father S. Kuldip Singh Sodhi, who inspires me to live a truthful and simple life.

CONTENTS

	Acknowledgments	Page i
	Introduction	Page 01
Chapter I	Know Where Your Money Goes	Page 04
Chapter II	Expenses Should Not Exceed Income	Page 22
Chapter III	Set Your Goals and Objectives	Page 34
Chapter IV	Pay Yourself First	Page 42
Chapter V	Buy Excellent Businesses	Page 45
Chapter VI	Use Other People's Brains	Page 61
Chapter VII	Use Other People's Money	Page 66
Chapter VIII	The Skilled Investor Vs. The Lucky Gambler	Page 68
Chapter IX	Trying It All Together – My Parting Words	Page 71
	About The Author	Page 74

ACKNOWLEDGMENTS

This book was made possible by unconditional support from Sarah Berneche, Irene Merritt, Nishaan Sodhi, Coon Huey, Kassandra Fiore and Fabiana Ramos.

Thank you for all. I hope this book reflects your best hopes for me and the future our loving universe.

INTRODUCTION

Throughout the history of mankind, humans have used and reused many types of financial systems. We learn finance from our parents, friends, and colleges. The one thing most of us have learned is to chase after the one thing, money. And the rise of capitalism has the world singing one song, and one song only: *money, money, money, mooonneeeyy!* I believe in capitalism; I support it whole-heartedly. And because I do, I've found myself singing the same song once or twice before. Yet, as I've made strides throughout my career as a portfolio manager, I've found myself singing this song much less.

I'm here to speak to you about money, but not in the way you're accustomed to. Instead of focusing on lifting your material status, I want to show you how to lift your spirits and lead a blissful life using a dynamic, holistic financial approach. I'm equally invested in your financial portfolio as I am in your portfolio of values, knowing first-hand the search for riches often runs parallel to the search for meaning.

Before we talk money, I'd like to show you my tantric side. Perhaps you live in a comfortable home. Perhaps you have air conditioning. You probably never dread dealing with pesky houseflies or mosquitos! You drive an automatic car with an excellent stereo system and leather seating; it takes you wherever your family wants to go. Your fridge is always stocked, so you never worry about having enough to eat, and you rarely give much thought to your daily shower, while some others in the world are desperate for clean drinking water.

The orange juice you drink with your breakfast is plentiful; you never need to ration it or worry whether you'll have enough for tomorrow. When Mom roasts a delicious chicken for dinner, stuffed with lemons and fragrant garlic, your children don't fight for the last piece of the chicken at the table. You're a Canadian citizen, and like most Canadian citizens, life is good.

When it comes to your lifestyle in general, we can conclude you're living a significantly better life than most of the world's population. Since your life is arguably better than that of so many others, you might wonder why you need to read my *bakwaas*[1] at all.

Well, here it is. Truthfully, you have a nice car, nice house, and everything is plentiful, but you may not realize this on a *conscious* level. Like many wealthy people, you probably spend a significant amount of your precious time wondering and worrying about money. I want you to think beyond the value of a dollar and peer into the value of your life's portfolio.

My goal for this book has two-fold: to share my experiences as a professional financial advisor and to simplify the complex subject of managing your money. In *"Fooled by Randomness,"* Nassim Nicholas Taleb, explains how "$10 million earned through Russian roulette does not have the

---

[1] Baakwas: A Hindi term for nonsense

same value as $10 million earned through the diligent and artful practice of dentistry" (Marks, 162). What is the difference between the lucky gambler and the skilled investor? The skilled investor takes the long view, embodying determination, certainty, knowledge, reality, the law, and market outperformance.

Whereas, the lucky gambler chases randomness, probability, belief, theory, anecdotes, and survivorship bias. Ultimately, becoming a skilled investor involves patience and doing the work. Though it takes some effort, understanding the difference between lucky breaks, skilled investing will give your family more time to spend on the real human issues at hand, such as the health of your mind, body, and spirit.

CHAPTER I:
KNOW WHERE YOUR MONEY GOES

Have you ever sat down and thought about where your money goes? If you haven't, that's okay. I mean why should you. It all seems so simple, right? First, the money enters into your bank account. Next, you use it to purchase coffee, clothes, and cars, etc. You may choose to set some aside or spend it all. Maybe you budget so you know exactly how much money is in your bank account, as well as how it all gets divided.

I'm afraid in reality it's just not that simple. The budgets get revised few times a year to clarify the spending habits and devise new plans for achieving the financial goals. I have a different approach to budgeting, and it involves more than just crunching numbers.

LISTING THE MINOR EXPENSES

Before you begin, it's important that you have some sense of your general spending and expenses, including your essentials such as mortgage payments or rent, electricity, insurance, and gas bills and food. Once the major, unavoidable expenses are out of the way, we can focus on saving money for your non-major expenses.

Fill out Step 1 to the best of your ability.

Step I

a) Monthly mortgage payments or base rent: _____

b) Average monthly electricity payment: _____

c) Average monthly gas payment: _____

d) Average monthly water expense: _____

e) Monthly grocery budget: _____

f) Monthly daycare or childcare costs: _____

g) Monthly transportation costs, including car insurance, gas, and other expenses: _____

h) Monthly entertainment budget (Restaurant meals, concerts, etc.): _____

i) Monthly spending on gifts and other miscellaneous items: _____

j) Monthly spending on clothing and accessories: _____

Total Monthly Expenditures: _____

When it comes to budgeting, for many people, the buck starts *and* stops here.

Contrary to popular belief, I truly think that when it comes to setting an effective budget, these are the last things you need to account for. I'm not saying that knowing how much you spend on the essentials isn't important, but in the long run, it is counter-productive to emphasize them so strongly.

In extreme cases, like that of my friend Raj, it can be nothing but a waste of your time and energy.

RAJ – THE FRUITLESS BUDGETER

Let me tell you about a close friend of mine named Raj. With remarkable consistency, Raj has participated in this budgeting exercise for the past 35 years. That's almost his whole working life! He has his two kids who are studying abroad and send him weekly reports of their expenses. *Do you know what Raj does?* He yells at his adult children for spending too much on coffee in a month. Has the yelling been effective? Of course is hasn't. In fact, this exercise, if you ask me, has done nothing to strengthen his family's financial health. Instead, it has created a false value system and unnecessary tension and hostility.

Young adults in university and college are bound to incur many expenses, which I believe have little use being accounted for. By accounting for them, at Raj's request, his two children when becoming adults will fret over spending $5 a day on coffee - over the long term, is not only a waste of time but definitely not worth the mental stress!

What can I say, I like my coffee.

So if I don't recommend budgeting, then what? This is where defensive budgeting comes in to play.

DEFENSIVE BUDGETING

Through defensive budgeting, I'll show you a few tricks to give you the *real* information you need for effective budgeting. Defensive budgeting is an enhanced, more skillful approach to budgeting. Rather than regularly budgeting for major expenses and petty cash, it will encourage you to acquire the necessary knowledge for managing the expenses portion of your cash flow. For this to work as well as possible, it's important you follow these instructions as best as you can. It won't take long until you're taking a walk down Easy Street.

Defensive budgeting involves getting a handle of the three *Terrible I's* – Income Tax, Interest, and Insurance. In order to maximize this exercise, you're going to need a blank cheque and a pen.

THE FIRST TERRIBLE I – Income Tax

1. Take your chequebook and pull out a blank cheque. On it, write down the approximate amount of your family's monthly gross income — almost as if you are writing a real cheque.

2. Hold this cheque in your hands, and slowly tear off a quarter of it. This quarter represents your family's biggest expense in Canada. I call this the first *Terrible I*. This first I — **Income tax** — is dreaded, and rightfully so.

3. Next time you add your weekly grocery bills to your budget, use some of that time instead to inform yourself on how you can cut some of your income tax expenses. A little effort here will lead to fresh ideas for saving money, and eventually to tangible results.

Although cutting spending on weekly groceries or utilities is often out of the question, the same isn't true for how much you spend on your income tax.

A FEW TIPS FOR SAVING ON INCOME TAX

The Canadian government's tax policies are designed to benefit the public at large. Your income tax rate is no different. Through taxes, you pay your fair share to the country so it can do its part in running the country's affairs and contribute to a better future for all of our citizens.

When it comes to saving on tax, self-employment is one option that I believe works out well both for individuals in the beginning and for the long-term, and also aligns with goals of the country and its policy makers. If married, maybe one of the spouses should venture out into this lucrative, simple (definitely not easy) employment.

If you are skeptical and believe self-employment is risky, please understand that your job, though it may seem stable, carries the same risks. Of course, there is the risk of losing your job or not getting the promotion you were hoping for. While being self-employed doesn't carry the same risks, it has a few advantages that make it worth putting in the effort and starting your own business. This is because when you're self-employed, many items are tax deductible:

1. **Car Use:** Depreciation, gas, parking, toll route, repairs, and maintenance.

2. **Communication:** Mobile phone, the Internet, etc.

3. **Your Home:** From heating to property insurance, the portion of your home used for carrying out your business is included.

4. **Entertainment:** Restaurants to meet with clients, meals eaten out can be listed as business expenses.

5. **Supplies and subscriptions:** This includes website and magazine subscriptions along with basic supplies including pencils, paper, printers, etc.

Small businesses are, by far, the leaders in job creation in our economy. At the end of the day, even if many taxpayers exaggerate these items and take advantage of the deductions, it is still as good for the nation as it is for the taxpayer; the extra money in the pocket of business owners provides more room for the survival and growth of everyone else. I recommend taking advantage of these generous offers from the Canadian Revenue Agency and becoming a job provider instead of a job seeker.

If self-employment is not for you, there is still a lot that you can do to save on income taxes. Here are a few tips that many people fail to consider.

1. **Split income with your children over the age of 14:** Pay them for babysitting their younger siblings and deduct the allowable amount from lower income spouse.

2. **Maximize Registered Retirement Savings Plan (RRSP):** Especially if your total debt is less than your family's total annual income.

3. **Use a Tax-Free Savings Account (TFSA),** to protect from investment income taxation.

4. **Prioritize capital gains:** and Canadian qualified dividends over interest income in your non-registered investment accounts.

5. **Use a Registered Disability Savings Plan (RDSP),** if any of your family members is qualified for disability tax credit. Canadians can get up to $90,000 in government

bonds and grants along with tax-deferred compounding through RDSP.

6. **Maximize a Registered Education Savings Plan (RESP)** for your children's post-secondary education savings. Canadian children up to the age of 17 can get up to $7,200 in Canadian education savings grant and up to $2,000 in government bond with added benefit of compounding their savings for up to 25 years in a tax-deferred environment.

7. **Negotiate with your employer to allow home or vehicle expenses if you think you use them for work.** By signing Canadian Revenue Agency's form T2200 (Declaration of Conditions of Employment), your employer is certifying that the employee met the conditions of employment and had to pay for the expenses under her employment contract. You can claim the expenses on your income tax return and have to keep records to support the claim.

Now that we've gotten a decent handle on Income Tax let's discuss the second Terrible I – Interest.

THE SECOND TERRIBLE I - Interest

1. Write 'Income tax' on the torn quarter and put it aside. Once again hold the remainder of the cheque in front of your eyes.

2. Tear off a third of the remaining cheque. This represents the second largest expense Canadians incur, and what I call the second *Terrible I*, or **Interest**.

From my experience in the financial planning industry, I can comfortably say that more than 80% of Canadians have some consumer debt on top of the mortgages they carry on their homes. Typically, 15-20% of your paycheque goes directly towards paying off the interest you've accumulated (and not because you bought coffee last week!)

A variety of different loans — including student loans, credit card debt, a line of credit, or car loans — can result in these debts. Although this *I* is a little smaller in size than the first one, managing the second *Terrible I* can play a *major* role in keeping everything at the top in order.

Easier said than done, right?

Managing interest isn't easy. Anyone in Canada who can accomplish this simple, but by no means, easy achievement of ridding themselves of all kinds of debt is on a place to have very good control of the remaining two *Is*.

MY APPROACH TO SAVING ON INTEREST

1. **Get a handle on family debt.** Acknowledge and accept that your debt is not only yours, but also belongs to your family. Sit with your family one evening or weekend afternoon and write down the numbers. Hiding debt is very dangerous and weakens family bonds.

2. **Craft a clear and realistic plan.** Put together a realistic pathway to achieve your ultimate financial objective, which ultimately should be to have zero personal debt. It doesn't matter how long the process takes to complete; it's important to have a clear vision and an action plan that you can commit to.

3. **Stop adding more debt.** Cut corners where you can and avoid adding new debt. Look for products and produce on sale at your grocery store, raid your pantry and freezer, and aim to make more meals at home. Brainstorm ways you can reduce your expenses without compromising the quality of your relationships. While I joke about coffee, try brew coffee, lattes, etc. at home instead of buying "coffee"

outside, especially if several individuals in your house like "coffee", this can add up to hundreds of dollars in savings a year.

4. **Consolidate as much as you can.** Seek professional help or shop around for the best rates possible on credit cards, mortgages, etc. Do your best to consolidate and normalize (2% to 3% above bank prime rate) interest expenses.

5. **Increase your family income.** If you have children, ask them to get a newspaper route, or babysit if they're of age. Older children should get a regular part-time or summer job; everyone should pitch in.

6. **Look for some form of self-employment.** For example, you could drive for Uber in your free time for extra money, or enlist your services on sites such as Upwork. As self-employed, some of your expenses can be tax deductible. If you were to drive for Uber, for example, you could write off your car lease payments, interest payments, insurance, gas, parking, and car maintenance. Depending on your work with freelance sites, you might be able to deduct Internet costs, cell phone bills, software, and so on. Self-employment is a great option to allow you to make more money while decreasing your present expenses.

THE THIRD TERRIBLE I - Insurance

1. Please write 'Interest' on the second piece of torn paper from your cheque and place it with the first 'income tax' portion of the cheque.

2. Once again, hold the remaining piece of the shortened cheque and tear off half of the remaining cheque.

3. This is your third biggest expense in Canada, what I call the third *Terrible I* — **Insurance**.

Human beings have an innate desire to make the most of the financial decisions based on two things: fear and greed. So, in fear of losing our beautiful lifestyles, we pay for many different forms of insurance protections. These include car insurance, home insurance, healthcare insurance, life insurance, employment insurance, and in some cases, insurance for our pets, TVs, and cell phones! This speaks more to fear than to faith and doesn't make strong financial sense.

Let's begin with life insurance. By just doing a little homework, we can simplify the amount and the type of life insurance protection we require. Despite this, most Canadians don't do their homework, and will happily sign on to committing bill payments for the rest of their lives, without devoting any real time or effort to understanding this important financial product.

Unfortunately, many of us lack clarity on simple insurance questions, such as the type of life insurance needed to match our needs, or whether or not we really need to insure our new television set.

AVOID INSURANCE PREMIUMS BY BEING SELF-INSURED

If you have something valuable and you're seeking financial compensation to protect you or your family's lifestyle in the event of loss or damage, then I would wholeheartedly recommend looking into an insurance agreement. However, these days people seem to be insuring items that truly don't warrant an insurance policy. Staying in line with our goals of decreasing insurance costs, we can make conscious decisions to become *self-insured*. Listed below are a few ways I've become self-insured with many everyday items that people are increasingly getting insured.

PERSONAL ITEMS

This includes: Jewellery, electronics, cameras, computers, cell phones, furnishings, etc.

I am not in favour of insuring any of these items, though your home insurance policy should actually cover some of them.

Instead, I'd like to introduce the simple concept of being *self-insured*.

SAVING ON CELL PHONES

I'm not soliciting any brand, but I've always used a Blackberry rather than an iPhone because the former is much sturdier. In place of buying insurance, I've always invested in protecting my phone with a solid Otter Box case. I've also never purchased the latest model, so I've always paid less than others. In the event of loss or damage, it will cost less to replace.

Prudent money management is very much about frugality. Sometimes it's important to pull yourself out of the rat race and differentiate yourself by making smart financial decisions.

SAVING ON COMPUTERS

My first laptop computer was from EPSON, and I paid more than $3,000; my last one is from IBM, and I paid less than $500. You can easily save money by purchasing refurbished versions online from IBM, Apple, and so on. In the last 10 years, I've worked on the best machines at very little cost.

I understand the appeal in buying the newest and best item out in the market. However, these products often come with much higher costs and a greater fear of losing or damaging the equipment. Always keep in mind the value of the item in addition to the cost. You can definitely limit spending in this area and cut insurance needs on personal items to almost zero.

SAVING ON TRANSPORTATION

Car Insurance:

1. **Buy a used vehicle.** Most of the cars lose a significant percentage of their value within the first two years. Used vehicles are less expensive and cheaper to insure.

2. **Avoid making claims.** You pay premiums and are entitled to all financial compensation, but you are much better off financially, paying small repairs out-of-pocket and keeping your records super clean.

3. **Go for a higher deductible.** It's very important for me to do my best to put my case, i.e., opting for the higher deductible for your car insurance.

My family has three cars and four drivers. Two of them — my son and my daughter — are under than 25-years-old are considered high-risk. We pay approximately $5,500 in insurance per year, which comes out to around 5% of my annual income. Many of my clients and family friends are in similar situations and also pay through their noses. Even if it's a lot of money, I give credit to my track record with my insurance company (over 25 years with the same company) with very few claims. Having high deductibles forced me to pay for small repairs from my own pocket and shop around for better and cheaper body shops, last but not least, it has pushed me to ignore small dents and scuffs.

Believe me, if you are starting a family or have teenage children, car insurance companies are going to increase their share of your annual income year after year. As the custodian of your hard-earned income, it's important you learn the ropes. Canadians have the notion that when we pay for insurance coverage, in the event of damage — minor or major — the insurance company is responsible for all the expense.

I am with you — for the most part. Big claims (over $2,000 dollars in my case), the insurance company should pay. For minor damages and repairs, I've found that I am better off paying from my own pocket. Unlike us, insurance companies love premiums and do not like to pay for claims. Insurance companies can choose not to renew coverage every year, and evaluate debits and credits. This process can easily increase our premiums or place us in a vulnerable position if they decline our coverage.

Here are some key benefits of keeping high deductible car insurance from my perspective:

1. Insurance companies have never declined me, and overall I've saved time, energy, and money.

2. A higher deductible is expensive, but I pay reasonable premiums for additional teenage drivers.

3. Because my family is aware of our need to pay out of pocket for fender benders, we are more cautious and, in my opinion, are better drivers.

4. We've learned to live with the appearance of used cars. Instead of prioritizing materialistic things, we care more about life and derive more meaning from simple things.

To note: high deductibles on claims also work well in the case of disability and medical benefits insurance.

If you are presently looking for long-term disability insurance, or find yourself interested in the future, the underwriting company will offer you different waiting periods before your claim starts, as well as different periods for the length of your benefits. To cut it short, I'll use the following example. Say I have to buy a long-term disability plan and my agent brings me three different options:

1. $4,000 per month benefits for 5 years, with a waiting period of 91 days. Annual premiums of $2,000.

2. $4,000 per month benefits for 10 years, with a waiting period of 365 days. Annual premiums of $1,500.

3. $3,500 per month benefits for 15 years, with a waiting period of 365 days. Annual premiums of $1,500.

I would go for option three.

Here are the reasons:

1. **I can afford to wait.** Drawn from my savings account, I strongly believe I can afford my lifestyle for at least one year. I can also cut some of my expenses. Avoid paying for something you can do yourself, such as self-insuring for one year.

2. **Age and life situation.** I am 50, and in the case of disability, I would prefer the insurance cover me for the longest period possible as opposed to receiving more money. For this reason, I'd opt for $500 less coverage in exchange for 5 more years of protection.

OTHER WAYS TO SAVE ON INSURANCE

1. **Shop for a reputable insurance company with great customer service.** Stick with them forever. I've always been with one insurance company and have all my coverage through one agent. By cultivating a rich, long-

term relationship, my family has undoubtedly reaped financial rewards.

2. **Better to be under-insured than over-insured.** When I bought a 7-year-old Chevrolet Impala, I only had comprehensive insurance. After a little consideration, I concluded that in the event of an accident, I could easily get it fixed or replace it with another used car. Do seek professional advice before acting, but this conviction has saved me a great deal of money from all types of insurance (including life insurance.)

3. **Forget extended coverage.** Last but not least, I am not in favour of extended coverage for new cars. If you can afford a $50,000 vehicle, you should be able to pay to replace or fix the transmission or another major part for $5,000. If you can't, you may be living beyond your means which ultimately will hinder your chances of getting rich.

I believe if you must pay premiums for medical or dental bills, you are better off having a high deductible. I don't want to look like philosopher or preacher, but I would still like to share something I strongly believe. Once you live without dental insurance or implement a high deductible, you will have an easier time adopting certain positive habits. You will brush your teeth more frequently, floss, or eat less sugary food. In my case, I incorporate Datun — the process of chewing and biting on a small wooden stick — at least twice a week with maple branch from my neighbourhood forest (while I take my dog for a walk, no less). I have no cavities, strong gums, and my teeth get a regular workout.

SAVING ON INSURANCE: LEARNING THE HARD WAY

After migrating to Canada in 1992, I joined a brokerage full-time as a life insurance sales person commonly referred to as an insurance advisor. Right after accepting the role with my brokerage, I started attending weekly learning sessions and became convinced of all the benefits of Universal Life Insurance. My first sale was to my sister-in-law and her husband. They had two kids and a mortgage. When the topic of life insurance came up, and they asked me to recommend a good policy, I wasted no time in promoting the benefits of Universal policies. My pitch was so good that my wife suggested she get one, too. Within the next few days, I signed all of them for 100K coverage with an approximately $50 monthly premium.

As with almost every pre-authorized payment, money kept moving from our account to the insurance company's account, and this lasted for five years. Like many others at the time, I thought the best way to create wealth was to buy cheap term life insurance and use the remaining left over money to invest in mutual funds. Eventually, something clicked, and I finally decided to do my homework. The first thing I did was I opted to cancel my wife's universal policy and sign up for a twenty-year term policy with a smaller premium and almost triple the coverage. I was bothered by the fact that the initial policy had less than $500 cash surrender value and felt cheated by my own ignorance and greed since commissions from universal life were significantly more than the term insurance policies.

To derive some valuable learning from the above experience, we must assume that if I had the option to return to 1993 and sign my wife up for a life insurance policy, there would have been many options and almost all of them better than the one we signed up for. Just adding extra coverage from her work group benefits — CIBC flexible benefits plan had the option to add life insurance coverage of up to three times her annual income — would have cost her only $9 per month in premiums. So the math would have looked like this:

Option A: What I originally chose

Cost of insurance we signed without any homework: $600/year for $100,000 coverage

Cost of optional insurance through group benefits: $108/year for $105,000 coverage

Option B: What I Should Have Chosen

Tax refund from contributing $600/year in RRSP: $200

Payments for $105,000 coverage through work: $108

Savings in hand: $92/year

The second option (through work benefits) is easy to understand and a more transparent option. It would have helped us become better savers and investors, instead of mere customers of an insurance company. Even without any growth we would have had $4,200 in our retirement savings seven years later, giving us a head start.

TYING TOGETHER THE TERRIBLE Is

Through the three *Terrible Is* – Income Tax, Interest, and Insurance, nearly 50% of your hard-earned income is slipping away before you even see it. Next time you spend your valuable time on activities such as budgeting groceries, be wise by elevating your understanding of Income Tax, Interest, and Insurance. How can you gain more control of these *Is*? Knowing the answer to this will benefit your family, perhaps better than knowing how much your daughter spent at Starbucks last Tuesday! And remember: the gift of looking after the three *Is* is simple, but also important knowledge you can pass on to future generations (all without accumulating estate tax.)

I can promise you that this solution is more likely to bring more financial freedom than the conventional inheritance so often sought after.

CHAPTER II:
EXPENSES SHOULD NOT EXCEED INCOME

"Annual income twenty pounds, annual expenditure nineteen six, result happiness. Annual income twenty pounds, annual expenditure twenty pounds ought and six, result misery." — **Charles Dickens, David Copperfield**

Many of us have been conditioned to believe that income and expenses should positively correlate, and focus more on acquiring increasingly extravagant items than on living with less stress. Think hard for a second about the people you know. Notice the cars they drive, the luxurious lunches they regularly enjoy, and the houses they live in. See all of the nice things they have? In some cases, you or other friends of theirs have inspired those purchases! This is called keeping up with the "Jones."

The dangerous thing with frivolous spending is that it can often lead to debt. People justify debt in the same way as students justify partying; "But everyone's doing it!" is how the familiar cry goes. Over time, irresponsible debt — just like irresponsible partying — will slowly but surely impact your overall quality of life.

While the thought of living below your means may not sound appealing, there are alternatives for adding meaning and value to your life that extend beyond conspicuous consumption.

A quick reality check on two primary components of your cash flow statement — income (cash inflows) and expenses (cash outflows) can put things into perspective. Up to a certain point, the income you earn from work is not something you can control. Incidents such as death, health issues, being laid off, or even retirement can also usher in abrupt change. However, you do have control over the other part of the equation — expenses.

While we're often quite conscious about controlling obvious, habitual expenses such as groceries, gas bills, or entertainment, we're not as critical about larger expenses. The primary expenses we really need to pay attention to; housing and transportation.

THE HIGH COST OF HIGH LIVING

A luxurious car and a big house can put a dent in your cash flow. A new, expensive and rapidly depreciating car and a larger and more expensive house aren't always necessary. This type of thinking and ensuing practices can impact other areas of your life in negative ways: more money spent to care for these items, more stress and worry, and higher utility bills. You'll also have less money to spend on experiences, such as travel, outings with your family, and activities with friends.

In today's world, you can drive a new luxury car with little effort. It's fairly simple to walk into a dealership and finance a brand new sports car. Instantly, your friends will see you as more successful, and you'll feel better about yourself for a bit. There's no doubt you'll *look* cool. However, I see things a bit differently. Your brand new sports car depreciates 25% right after you drive it off the lot. On top of that, you can add the following to your pre-existing list of monthly expenses: higher car insurance, premium (and therefore more expensive) gas, and higher expenses at the mechanic shop whenever you have a problem with your car. How can we mitigate frivolous spending?

WHEN IT COMES TO YOUR HOUSE, SIZE MATTERS

Homes — incidentally your largest expense — are often the most overlooked cost when it comes to overspending. From my experience, Canadians tend to live in much larger and more extravagant homes than they really need.

Fortunately, the appeal of downsizing and buying houses with smaller square footage is growing rapidly. Individuals are seeking to live within their means, pay off student debt, or simply experience more of what life has to offer, are opting to do without extra bedrooms, second living rooms, or superfluous closet space (which they'd only spend more money to fill.) This is seen especially in larger cities with the evolution of condo development. While smaller spaces may not appear as impressive, they come with a host of benefits worth considering.

People unnecessarily correlate small houses with some sort of negative feeling. However, this simply isn't true. Living in a smaller house offers many benefits:

1. **Cleaning is more convenient.** A smaller space equals less to clean, saving you both time and energy. You won't need to purchase cleaning products as frequently, and you can likely get by with a very basic vacuum and mop as opposed to more durable and expensive versions. It might even be worth your while to hire help in this area.

2. **You save money on clothing and other unnecessary items.** Because you don't have space to accommodate all of your wants, you will be more selective with what you purchase. This helps your bank account but also supports the earth. This might afford you the ability to support eco-friendly and sustainable designers, as you'll purchase fewer items.

3. **More time spent outdoors.** Close living quarters can certainly feel cramped at times, but this will encourage your family to spend more time outdoors hiking or ice skating, or simply spending more time together as a unit. This offers a healthy lifestyle.

4. **Money savings on utilities.** It is much less expensive to cover the utilities of a smaller dwelling as opposed to a larger one.

5. **Higher quality of life.** This one is arguable, but when you detach yourself from needing a larger house, you open up the possibility of living close to work or residing in a nicer neighbourhood. This might mean a shorter commute, more time spent with family and friends, and a more active lifestyle. You might also save on transportation costs and daycare if necessary.

Owning a home is not just about image. Consider your internal values; your home is, in many ways, an expression of those values. Would you prefer a large house to a truly value family, closeness, the environment, community, time, and happiness?

Interested in living a more heart-centred lifestyle? Here are a few questions to get you started.

1. How much space do you need to live comfortably? This can be in square footage or number of rooms. Consider

how layout variations might impact your decision, and be sure to anticipate any changes, such as future children or work-from-home arrangements.

2. What are you holding on to that you don't need? What can you donate or sell this week to make extra money and lessen your material load?

3. How would you spend or invest your money if your housing and transportation costs were to decrease?

4. How would your life change if your accommodation and transportation costs were much less?

5. How would a smaller dwelling impact your family dynamic?

6. How does it make you feel to give up the dream of a larger home?

7. How does living in a smaller space make you feel?

8. If you own a more expensive car, what value does it offer you? What would it mean if you traded it in for a less expensive version or started taking public transportation?

MOVE YOUR BODY, NOT YOUR HOUSE

It goes without saying, your house is your biggest asset and also your biggest expense. Managing this one expense prudently can take you far in terms of how efficiently you save and accumulate wealth. When it comes to being healthy, it's important to keep your body moving. But when it comes to being financially healthy, the opposite is true with your house!

Once upon a time, it was considered financially wise for young customers and new immigrants to Canada to view their first home as their final home. In today's economy, this is almost impossible. Instead, I'd suggest not making more than one move in your lifetime.

Canadians move at least 5 times, and each move costs approximately $50,000 — more if you calculate brokerage fees, land transfer tax, legal, and moving tax. These moving costs are not a required living expense, but an expense that can be avoided. As the average Canadian couple can save $50,000 after 3-4 years of hard work and the average working life for Canadians is approximately 40 years; excessive moving can result in the loss of a large percentage of a couple's life savings (approximately 15-20 years worth of savings.)

Your work, family situation, budget, and personal preferences all play a role in determining where you settle down. These should all be considered when making the initial decision. By picking the right place first, you'll save yourself a lot of hassle and money in the future, should you decide to move again.

My clients often come to me and tell me they want to move because they can sell their house for more than they paid for it, and make significant capital gains. On the surface, this sounds simple, but if you dig deeper moving it is a lot more expensive than you may think.

To illustrate this, let's say we wanted to buy and sell our principal house in Toronto area. As of May 2016, the average price of a home in the city is $783,000. Now, this is the cost of the property and does not include the cost of the move.

On top of this we can add:

- Realtor commission (5.0%)
- HST on commission (13%)

- ☐ Land Transfer Cost (2.7%)
- ☐ Legal Fees (Approximately $1,500)
- ☐ Movers (Approximately $1,000)

With these numbers, the cost of moving would be rough:

- ☐ Realtor: $39,150
- ☐ HST: $5,090
- ☐ Land Transfer Cost: $21,141
- ☐ Legal Fees: $1,500
- ☐ Movers: $1,000

Total moving cost, on top of the price of a new house: $67,880

In essence, you're paying $67,880 more than originally anticipated. Let's say you move three times in 20 years — that's over $200,000 just in added (and often unaccounted for) moving costs! With the average Canadian earning roughly $50,000 a year before taxes, it would take nearly four years of work just to pay off the realtor, HST, land transfer cost, legal fees, and moving costs.

This is why it is extremely important to carefully choose your initial home purchase, and make sure you move into a place where you can see yourself living in for the long term. Not only will it save you the hassle of moving, but tons of money as well.

Similarly, not moving actually adds to the value you take from life. Neighbours, friends, community living, and a sense of belonging are all abundant when you stay where you are. Remaining in the same home allows you to build relationships with others, strengthen bonds, and create meaning. This isn't to say you can't do this elsewhere, but each time you move you compromise the quality of these intangibles. Each move must be pitted against any foreseeable losses, such as:

- Fewer interactions with family
- Lost friends
- Added stress (moving, finances, meeting new people, learning the ropes in a new community)
- Fewer connections

The human mind is designed to grow infinitely and likes to take advantage of any opportunity. However, when you plan to raise a family which determines your choice of long-term accommodations, I believe the mindset should be that this is the city or area you will live in forever — or at least until retirement. This mindset will give you a lot of clarity and add important considerations, like the school district, proximity to work, family, public amenities like hospitals, highways, grocery stores, and so on before finalizing the decision. Big financial decisions like home buying fueled by lofty thought processes do nothing other than creating ongoing changes in plans costing a lot of time and energy. My suggestion is to plan for the best option, which is assuming your first home is going to be your final home. As I mentioned earlier, at least this mindset will reduce your house hopping from an average of five times to less than two, and will add a lot of value to your future financial health.

While greater job opportunities sometimes await elsewhere, these are important considerations. This principle is one of my favourites, because it has ultimately helped me to become more cost-wise.

WHY DRIVE FAST WHEN YOU CAN DRIVE FRUGAL?

When it comes to your expenses, transportation will often be your second largest – so it's important to be smart about what you drive. Like owning a smaller home or condo, a smaller, more fuel-efficient car will require less expenditures on gas and will often have far cheaper repairs. On top of this, it will get you from Point A to Point B just as well as if you took the pricier option. Sure, you may not look as *cool*, but I think the added capital in your bank account is well worth the sacrifice. If you live in an urban area, you can completely avoid this expense by taking public transit. If you're in a relationship, a single car between the couple or an auto-share plan may work just as well. My point here is, don't just buy the fancy car for the sake of having a fancy car. At the end of the day, transportation is about getting where you need to be. If you can do this while saving money, why wouldn't you?

Far too many people today are wrongly ashamed of being labeled as frugal, or advocates of frugal living. But you'll find that in doing so and embracing the frugal ideology, you will save a lot of unnecessary stress and avoid the never-ending rat race of *who has the nicer things*. On top of this, you'll find that the money in your bank account piles up over time.

MR. SPENDER – A STORY OF FRUGAL TO FANCY TO FRUGAL AGAIN

"There is no dignity quite so impressive, and no independence quite so important, as living within your means." — **Calvin Coolidge**

Mr. Spender is an immigrant from India currently residing in Canada. Not many people would think that by importing Indian dresses to Canada, you could create a profitable business. Well, Mr. Spender did just that and made a lot of money doing it. He is extremely well connected in India and has garnered many loyal friends and suppliers back home. As a personable and intelligent individual, he has established an excellent business selling Indian dresses upon arriving in Canada. He researched his market meticulously and made advantageous deals with Indian dress suppliers back home. His dedication began to pay off after a few years of breaking even. He began to make millions running the Indian dress store, which I strongly applaud him for. His business strategy is one that many have tried to replicate, but trying to imitate Mr. Spender's work ethic is a difficult task.

After years of successfully running his Indian dress business, Mr. Spender was presented with an opportunity to sell his business for a large sum of money. The buyer was a fellow Indian man who was willing to pay a lot for Mr. Spender's reputable company. Although Mr. Spender valued his business highly, his passion for running the store has decreased, so he made the decision to sell the business with the intention of finding a new passion.

Mr. Spender became an avid golfer once his store was sold. Seamlessly he played the sport hours upon hours a day. There was a popular saying that goes, "if you cannot score under 100 after two years of golfing then golf is not your business, and if you can do it, then you have no business." Mr. Spender was in the second category. In fact, he accomplished this in under six months. Golf consumed most of Mr. Spender's time, but as all Toronto golfers know, the sport only lasts six months a year. When golf season finished, Mr. Spender had to divert his energy into something new. This left him with two options: to go looking for new relationships and travel, or resort to his entrepreneurial instincts. He chose the latter and started a business once again.

Mr. Spender started importing office chairs and hardware from China to sell in Canada. I was perplexed when he told me about his new venture. He abandoned his suppliers and entered a completely new market. This venture quickly floundered. While I am not sure whether it was that he lost his passion, or if it was simply the wrong business, I could see Mr. Spender's work ethic diminished. He was making new, extremely wealthy friends on the golf course and slowly felt drawn to the expensive cars and Rolex watches, expressions of their tangible successes. These new friends marveled at their own lists of achievements, and in my opinion, were egotistical gamblers.

Investors in the 1990s made plenty of easy money (in the short term) by trading technology stocks. Mr. Spender was one of these investors and was overly confident that these stocks would continue rising. One day Mr. Spender organized a poker game at his house and invited many of his colleagues from the golf course. I remember one of his friends only agreed to come if Mr. Spender served blue label Johnnie Walker scotch, to which he happily obliged. As everyone began to arrive, many of us started a conversation regarding technology stocks. In the middle of the conversation, Mr. Spender left the poker room abruptly and returned ten minutes later. After his return, we decided to start the poker game.

Mr. Spender appeared anxious. He rose from his seat several times to leave the room, only to return minutes later. He was the first one eliminated from the poker game - naturally, I was expecting a look of disappointment accompanying this loss, but instead a sinister looking smile crept over his face. Mr. Spender was smiling, as he explained because he had just made $1,000 by buying 1000 shares of Nortel at $87 and selling them an hour later for $88. He added that his understanding of trends associated with Nortel was strong enough for him to dignify buying 1000 shares. He believed Nortel stocks usually traded at their highest price around 3:30 pm, which was the time he sold the stocks. It became glaringly obvious that Mr. Spender arranged this poker game to show off to his friends by making quick money - a far cry from the man who once ran a million dollar business by working hard. Mr. Spender continued to invest all the money he made from selling his Indian dress business into technology stocks. Like many others, sadly Mr. Spender did not escape the technology bust. He lost his millions to greed.

Greed and desire can devour the good among human beings. Mr. Spender had forgotten what had made him rich and successful in the first place: hard work. He believed that with more incoming money, he has to spend more. This belief goes against my principle of "as income goes up, expenses don't have to." Easy money is very addictive, just like gambling and alcohol, and it can overpower you. On top of that, it represents the qualities of the lucky idiot — not the skilled investor.

CHAPTER III:
SET YOUR GOALS AND OBJECTIVES

"A goal properly set is halfway reached." – **Zig Ziglar**

Any journey is almost half complete the second you actually start it. This means making a committed effort to complete it, not just thinking about it! With that being said, putting your long-term life goals or short-term objectives into written goals on a piece of paper will do you wonders. Financially, these goals can be as straightforward as paying off your mortgage in 10 years.

I believe in a 6-step approach to achieving your goals, as written below.

1. Write down your goals and deadlines

Specific goals are more effective than broad goals. For example, "I aim to lose 5lbs over the next 60 days" is more effective than "I want to lose weight." In speaking of your holistic financial picture, this can be whatever you feel will enhance your family's life better financially, relationship-wise, or health-wise.

This is the easiest stage to execute, and it is really as simple as picking up a pen and paper and writing down a sentence. Some goals to consider:

- Saving 10% of your annual income for the next five years.
- Paying off a student loan of $50,000 within five years.
- Reducing credit card interest by calling your current provider this weekend or looking into alternatives.

2. Educate Yourself

Thanks to the Internet, you can pull out effective information from the comfort of your own living room. Researching and reading will give you some new ideas and also clarify other elements of a good goal setting process.

3. Specificity

Since you've done 40% of the work, let's build on that by becoming more specific with our goals. Achieving financial independence must include details like paying off your mortgage, clearing your other personal debts, or saving for children's educations (and how you're planning on funding this.) On top of this, look into all options, such as saving in advance, scholarships, extra cash, and study loans. This is of utmost importance.

4. Measurable Goals

Quantifying helps to add sense to your goals and objectives, and also helps in the next step. For example, if you'd like to get stronger, track your progress. Perhaps you'll find you can perform bicep curls with 25lb dumbbells at the beginning of your training, but six months in you're lifting 50lbs. This is an example of a measurable goal.

Many middle-aged Canadians would like to lose some body weight. To make this goal achievable, let's put down some numbers in a simple way: I am 30 pounds overweight. If I can burn an extra 300 calories by walking 1-hour everyday, and reduce my caloric intake by another 150, then I am losing approximately 50 grams of fat daily (100 grams of fat is 900 calories). If I can do that for 8 days, I will be 1 pound lighter. To achieve my goal of losing 30 pounds, I will need to stick to my routine for a minimum of 240 days.

My nutritionist friend, Sarah, prefers to measure health in more holistic terms. Instead of focusing on the weight issue, she encourages clients to address every aspect of their lives. Chronic stress, sleep, negative relationships, eating psychology, environmental factors, nutrient deficiencies, a sedentary lifestyle, allergies, inflammation, hormonal imbalances, and so on may all contribute to unwanted weight gain and assorted health issues.

While Western society idealizes and privileges thinness, the restriction and deprivation characteristic of all diets frequently leads to bingeing and overeating. Though many of us believe the latter are due to lack of willpower or discipline, bingeing and overeating are in fact biological and very normal responses to semi-starvation. The Dr. Ancel Keys Starvation Experiment (1944-45), where thirty-six young men deemed of superior health were starved (averaging 1,570 calories per day — the same amount as that of the modern male diet) and re-fed (3,000+), illustrates this phenomenon quite well.

In Chapter I, I discussed the importance of looking to the three *Terrible Is* — Insurance, Interest, and Income tax — instead of curbing minor expenses such as coffee. Similarly, Sarah feels calorie counting is an abysmal, overrated, and dangerous practice, and instead recommends adhering to the following:

- **Keep a consistent bedtime, ideally between 10-11pm.** Going to bed later than 11 pm can stress out the body and trigger the fight-or-flight response, as you're awake when you should be asleep. Going to bed later than 11 pm may also compromise sleep quality, and lead to increased cravings for sugary foods high in unhealthy fats.

- **Fill half your plate with non-starchy vegetables.** Forget the calorie savings; filling up on vegetables, either raw or cooked, will keep your energy levels up, support healthy digestion, and supply your system with much-needed vitamins, minerals, antioxidants, and fibre. Set an example for your children by serving vegetables with every meal and as snacks throughout the day, but resist the urge to pressure them.

- **Develop a system for coping with stress.** Make an effort to get up earlier to stretch or exercise, drink a glass of water with 2 tbsp. of lemon juice (the juice of 1/2 a lemon), and visualize. Start slowly. Take a 20-minute walk or try meditating for 5 minutes. Reading, journaling, preparing a nourishing breakfast, or deep breathing are also productive ways of managing stress and cutting through overwhelm.

- **Spend time with loved ones.** Women, in particular, relieve stress by tending-and-befriending or talking things out with friends. Schedule coffee or lunch dates, or join a book club. Group fitness classes are always a great idea too.

- **Find an exercise you enjoy doing.** Exercise is a great way to improve body composition, boost mood, and relieve stress. It's important to keep a strong body into old age, but in order to do so, you need to find an exercise you like to do. Sarah suggests trying a variety of workouts. Do you like working out solo, or would you prefer the guidance and support of classes? Do you feel more comfortable being anonymous at large gym, or would you prefer a boutique studio where everyone knows your name? Do you naturally gravitate to yoga and pilates, or does an energizing metabolic conditioning class appeal to you? All movement matters.

- **Eat when you are hungry and stop when you are full.** While "taste hunger" — the desire to eat something when you are not hungry — is perfectly fine, try to focus on eating only when you are hungry, chewing your food thoroughly, eating slowly, and being mindful of fullness. You'll find this practice of slowing down and savouring your food is more beneficial than counting calories or worrying whether food is wholesome. Sometimes you will be very hungry, while other times you may not have much of an appetite. This is all part of normal eating. By honouring your hunger and tuning into your body's signals, you can prevent the discomfort of overeating and derive more satisfaction from your meals simultaneously.

- **Instead of weighing yourself, measure your progress in other ways.** How is your energy on a scale of 1-10 with 10 being the highest? Are you sleeping 7-9 hours a night? Are you happy? How is your mood? How many push-ups can you perform correctly? Focusing on these markers rather than the number on the scale will ultimately prove more fulfilling than focusing on weight and body size.

Similarly, Warren Buffett looks at the big picture in terms of his health. Instead of micromanaging his food choices, he enjoys a glass of Coca-Cola and a few candies regularly as part of a healthy lifestyle. We must not only look at the numbers and labels on our food choices but the value they offer to our lives. As Sarah believes, all foods fit.

5. Set Realistic Goals

Setting realistic goals and having a strategy to achieve your goals go hand-in-hand.

We all have goals. Where we differ is based on the type of goals that we have. For instance, Bob, a 20-year-old college student, wants to make a million dollars before his 30th birthday. Sarah, a friend of Bob's, may have the same goals. However, she may be more strategic and realistic about how she will achieve the goal.

Sarah may devise a plan that involves saving, investing, working long hours, and not spending money on unnecessary items. Bob's goal may involve just getting a high paying job or winning the lottery. Who do you think has a more realistic shot at achieving their goal?

When it comes to your goals, it's important to ensure that they are realistic based on the strategy you've come up with. If one of the two components are lacking, you're setting yourself up for failure – something no one likes!

A realistic goal that many Canadians have is paying off their debt. When I say this goal is realistic, I mean it really is *realistic*. Sure you can pay off your debt, but do you have a strategy? Let's look at how this goal can be accomplished with a strategy.

Assume your family's gross annual income is $150,000 and your total debt is approximately $450,000.

- **If your income is less than your debt, then you need to take a step back and consider which assets you can sell to bring it under the threshold.** This may include moving to a smaller dwelling, ditching extra cars (therefore eliminate lease or car payments, insurance, gas, and repairs/maintenance), or learning to live with fewer vacations, shopping trips, and costly entertainment.

- **Increasing income is another option, such as doing part-time work.** Be mindful of this; make sure you still have time for your health and family. Otherwise, you are paying more than what you're earning in many ways.

- **Once you consolidate all debts into one or two segments, begin doing something we usually don't do at all — turning your mind into a fool.** Start paying your installments biweekly rather than monthly, which will give you two extra payments per year towards your debt. After a little back-of-the-envelope budgeting and trying to find some extra cash, talk to your banker and increase your installments by 5% to 10%. One way is to reduce amortization on your mortgage.

- **Complete one final task. Write down your plan in bold letters, sit with your family, and sign the document along with every other family member.** You'll commit to saving or raising $22,500 in one year by making a little more every week from odd jobs, such as shoveling snow, lawn mowing, dog walking, baby sitting, or paper delivery in the neighbourhood. Above all, it will make your family debt-free within 9 years.

Our goals here are realistic. Without counting on any raises, your family will earn approximately 1.3 million in the next 9 years — and you're only aiming to kill a beast weighing $450,000. Our plan is simple to understand and not difficult to implement. Instead of looking to hit the jackpot, we're planning to make a little extra dough from simple, but easily available daily jobs.

Lastly, even if we don't achieve what we aimed for, it will be a fun journey and will bring your family closer (and perhaps more wealthy.) Rest assured, your family will reap great benefits just by cultivating good habits and believing debt is no less than a sin as it is presented in the Old Testament.

6. Celebrate

Let us not take things so seriously. Whenever you achieve a goal, celebrate it. It can be as simple as taking your spouse out for dinner or movie or taking a vacation. The celebration does wonders in our mindset for good and healthy achievements and will guarantee our success.

CHAPTER IV:
PAY YOURSELF FIRST

"Don't save what is left after spending; spend what is left after saving." — **Warren Buffett**

I want you to consider the cheque you tore up earlier. This will clarify one of the biggest issues I see when it comes to saving. It's very simple, but from my experience, the majority of people — even if they may know and understand on a conscious level — still hesitate to act on it.

What is the problem? We all like to be the last beneficiary of our paycheque. This is not selfish. Each of us spends decades making money and giving it away to Income Tax, Interest, and Insurance, in addition to other living needs and wants, prior to paying ourselves. I'm very adamant about this belief. In the last 25 years, whenever a client of mine hears he or she might lose his or her job due to company restructuring and downsizing, their first instinct is to cease pre-authorized savings payments. They're cutting themselves off first before they cut anyone else off, such as cell phone companies, cable, or similar expenses.

In the money management world, when an individual achieves success and comes close to financial independence, some of their success may be attributed to the following basic principle:

10% of your paycheque goes to yourself — towards your long-term savings vehicles, such as RRSPs and TFSAs.

Cultivating this habit is pretty easy for beginners in the workforce or in the business world. 10% isn't an extraordinary amount, so it's do-able by the vast majority. Since this demographic generally doesn't have significant family obligations, such as mortgage payments or family expenses, it is easier to say 'YES!' and commit to it. Financial advisors find it very easy to ask for an increase in savings year after year as per their increase in income because they're already in the habit of paying themselves first. The raise they achieve will go, seamlessly, toward some of their savings.

If you're in the middle of your working life and missed the chance to cultivate this habit, below, you'll find suggestions to assist you in developing the difficult but important habit of paying yourself before others.

First: you must *start*. When I say start, I mean starting with any amount. Let's say you begin with 3% of your paycheque. Within a couple of years, you will not miss any of that 3%, and won't see any change in your lifestyle. So take that opportunity to increase your savings from 3% to 4.5%. Repeat this technique again until you've reached the goal of 10% of your paycheque.

This process could look something like this:

Years 1-3: 3%
Years 3-5: 4.5%
Years 5-7: 6%

Years 7-8: 8%
Years 8-10: 10%

By conditioning yourself over time, you'll become a far better saver in the long term.

The next part involves knowing where to invest your savings once you've built up some cash. What do you do with those savings to achieve something substantial in your life? To answer, here comes my fifth principle of money management: buying excellent businesses.

CHAPTER V:
BUY EXCELLENT BUSINESSES

"You must thoroughly analyze a company, and the soundness of its underlying businesses, before you buy its stock; you must deliberately protect yourself against serious losses; you must aspire to "adequate," not extraordinary, performance." — **Benjamin Graham, The Intelligent Investor**

I have two core beliefs pertaining to long-term investments. The first: simple investing, better living. The second belief involves never losing money and never forgetting this rule. While reading this chapter on buying excellent businesses, my approach may sound overly simplistic. But I'm keen to offer opinions that I deem easy-to-understand, implement, and monitor. I take principle protection seriously, but I also wish to put your hard-earned money to work.

Hopefully, you're on the same page regarding both the simplicity and protection of your savings from losses and that you're also prudent enough to develop the habit of paying yourself first. Let's assume again that for the last calendar year your family's gross income was $150,000 and that you've paid yourself first; you're able to devote $15,000 of your income toward a long-term savings vehicle, such as an RRSP.

Now, my experience has shown the majority of us will invest time and effort to engage the current economic conditions and try to match up with different sorts of investments available in the marketplace. Countless times I've heard, "Well the interest rates are rising to 50 basis, the best company to invest in for the next quarter is *Bob's Bananas*", or something along those lines.

Even if you have a professional advisor on board to help you to make better investment decisions, unfortunately, he or she will go through the same dilemma, probably at least once a year.

Nothing gives you more principal protection — and therefore, some peace of mind — than putting your money into fixed deposits with a leading banking institute. Placing money into vehicles such as Guarantee Investment Certificates (GICs) falls under both of my investment principals — simple and principle protection. At least that's what it appears on the surface when you put your money into GICs.

This is far from the actual truth.

Here's a simple example. If you invest all of your savings into a GIC with 3% guaranteed interest rate, through simple calculations using the rule of 72, your $15,000 will double in approximately 24 years, and you will have $30,000. Unfortunately, with inflation, the buying power of $30,000 will be much less than today's $15,000, and to me, it seems like a guaranteed loss. For the average investor, the only other option involves getting into the stock market directly or through some kind of mutual fund.

Mutual funds are not my favourite because of their high management expense ratios and payout structure for a portfolio manager, who is rewarded mostly on the basis of their quarter-to-quarter performance. This leads to a big disconnect from the real objective of investing in public companies. It goes without saying that paying additional fees will reduce your overall return. Assets with the highest returns also tend to have the lowest ancillary fees. Mutual funds, as a whole, are known to have comparatively high fee structures. Right off the bat, there are two types of fees that you will generally encounter with a mutual fund: Sales Charges, Management Fees, and Operating Expenses.

1. Sales Charges

Sales charges, otherwise known as loads, are fees that are charged when units of a fund are bought or sold. Sales charges are typically in the form of Front-End or Back-End Loads. Front-end loads involve paying a fee when shares in the fund are purchased. These fees can be up to 5% of the total value. It's easy to see why investment advisors would want to sell you mutual funds when they are earning commission!

Back end load fees are typically a higher percentage than front-end loads and can be as much as 6%. Through back-end loans, mutual fund companies incentivize investors to hold their funds for longer by decreasing the amount of the load the longer that the fund has been held in the portfolio.

Funds also exist with no load fee structures. This means that in some cases, you can buy a mutual fund without being charged when shares are bought or sold. It goes without saying that this is preferred, but the fund's performance and its overall MER (Management Expense Ratio) must be considered before making a decision.

2. Management Fees and Operating Expenses

The Management Expense Ratio (MER) is a term that is often used when comparing the fees of one mutual fund to another. MERs consist of two things: management fees and operating expenses. MERs typically range somewhere between 1% and 3% and are paid to the fund management company. Management fees encompass all direct expenses incurred in managing the investments. These include hiring the portfolio manager as well hiring a company to administer the fund.

Operating expenses reflect the day-to-day expenses of the fund. These may include bookkeeping, administration fees, filings with provincial securities commissions, legal fees, audit fees, custodian fees, and more. MERs are a sum of the management fees and operating expenses and are based on the total dollar amount invested in the company. It's important to keep them at the forefront of your investment decision!

WHO BENEFITS MOST FROM MUTUAL FUNDS – YOU OR THE MANAGER?

I stay away from mutual funds because I'm a long-term investor, plain and simple. My ideal investment horizon is *forever*, and with that in mind, I don't mind if my holdings experience is subpar over a quarter or a year — so long as the business fundamentals remain strong.

Often, I find that my long-term mindset contradicts with those running mutual funds. Big mutual fund Portfolio Managers get paid in two parts; their base salary and a quarterly bonus based on the performance of the fund in comparison to a previously established benchmark.

On the surface, this may seem like a good thing. After all, if you do well you should get rewarded, right? But if you dig a little deeper its apparent that this immediate reward system forgoes material long-term gains for smaller short-term ones.

I'll illustrate this with an example.

Let's suppose I am a portfolio manager with a big mutual fund company named Example Investments. And let's say that my compensation is directly linked to my quarterly performance, and not, say, my 5-year track record.

As I start the fund, I have an initial set budget of $1 billion. I use that to establish holdings in ten excellent businesses in possession of great business fundamentals, which I'm confident will be successful in the future.

The fund launches on January 1st, 2017 and by March 31st, 2017 all of my positions are performing very well except for one, which has been impacted by natural disasters out of its control. Because it has performed poorly, I may be inclined to drop it for another stock that may not be as good overall but will perform better over the next quarter or year.

In the next year, another one of my excellent businesses has been impacted by external events and hasn't been performing as well as it should in comparison to the benchmark. Again, I may drop it in favour of a business I believe will do well in the next quarter, regardless of long-term prospects.

In one short year, my portfolio has gone from ten great businesses to owning eight great businesses, and two that I suspect will perform well in the short-term. Over time this trend will continue to a point where I'm no longer buying ownership in excellent businesses, but instead playing a choosing game in hopes of being profitable over the next three months. The entire practice has shifted from investment to speculation.

Unfortunately, many mutual fund managers fall into the same cycle. Over time, their holdings don't result in long-term value creation, but rather, focus on incremental short-term gains. Warren Buffett, Prem Watsa, and many other investment gurus have amassed fortunes by focusing on a long-term strategy. In my opinion, real wealth is created through compound growth and long-term value creation. By constantly buying and selling holdings, it's impossible to establish any type of compound growth and very difficult to maintain an owners mindset.

So if not mutual funds, then what?

Well, before you invest in anything it's important to set a realistic return target for your savings. Now, you won't get anywhere near these returns by investing in GIC's or putting money into a savings account - but this is entirely possible by investing in an "excellent" business.

Excellent businesses are a lot easier to find than you may think. For instance, one of my favourite businesses is a company that everyone interacts with on a weekly basis. A quick glance around your house will show you why this is the case with Johnson & Johnson. Most of us are very familiar with and use Johnson & Johnson products including Tylenol, Visine, Band-Aids, Oral B, and Acuvue eye care products.

Johnson & Johnson is the world's second largest and perhaps the most diverse manufacturer of health care products. Mutual funds always boast about diversification, so let's see if we can achieve this important, but often overrated, attribute of a good investment. I will use the conventional five lens that financial literates commonly use to assess investment risks, or in our terms, principle protection. I will name and explain them, then relate them to J&J, hoping you will build confidence in knowing how to assess businesses.

1. **Business risk**

   Business Risk is the uncertainty of income flows. Pharmaceutical companies, whose revenue comes from a handful of drug manufacturing, maturity of patents life, or the emergence of new and better drugs, can lead to significant reduction in income. Since J&J has a diversified revenue stream, only 45% of total sales in 2015 were generated from the Pharmaceutical segment; the rest of the sales were from consumer and medical devices. Business risk, considering only patent expiry, is less than half than pure pharmaceutical business.

2. **Financial risk**

   Use Google Finance and pull out Johnson's 31 December 2015 balance sheet.

   - **No net debt on the balance sheet**
     With simple additions and subtractions, we conclude that J&J has no net debt on their balance sheet.

   - **Look for independently owned businesses**
     J&J has one of the best business models I have come across in my last 25 years of business analysis. Under J&J's umbrella, there are over 275 independent businesses. Now, the key word here is *independent* – so if any business goes through legal, financial, or business difficulties, the other 274 can breathe and perform normally. With respect to the whole company, there is a very little financial risk. Perhaps the least amount when comparing any other business I have analyzed.

3. Liquidity risk

Put simply; this means the certainty of converting share certificates into cash. There is decent trading in decent markets. J&J trades on the New York Stock Exchange and has approximately 2.7 billion widely held shares outstanding, an average approximated by many shares traded on an average trading day. J&J presents very little liquidity risk.

4. Country risk

J&J has established revenue streams in over 140 countries. In any given year, if a couple of those countries experience social or political unrest, have currency devaluation, a catastrophic event, or severe financial hardship, J&J will pass almost any stress test under any situation just from one of the best revenue diversification looking with country risk lens.

5. Exchange risk

As a Canadian investor, you can experience sharp volatility in your J&J pricing along with USD to CAD conversion. However, you shouldn't concern yourself or look for hedging strategies because, as per my recommendation, you want to take the long view. In this case, time will mitigate any currency exchange risk. With revenue streams from 140 countries, J&J naturally offers spectacular protection from currency exchange risk.

To sum it all up, Johnson & Johnson is a 135 year-old company doing business in more than 140 countries. Within J&J, there are more than 275 independent businesses. This business model of one company with 275 businesses along with a diversified revenue stream from hundreds of products gives Johnson & Johnson the much sought after principle protection. In reviewing the financial statements alone, we've concluded there's almost nil debt on their balance sheets and decades of an earning yield of around 8% - even during the tough economic periods like the 2008/2009 financial crisis.

My lucky number is 13; yours might differ. This is the number of businesses I aim to buy and hold for the long-term. If you can identify, and buy, 13 excellent businesses in the next 13 years — the solidity of them determined by a little bit of homework — you'll find yourself on a smooth ride towards your financial independence destination. As Warren Buffett has said, "it's far better to own a portion of the Hope diamond than 100 percent of a rhinestone". It may not take a linear shape, but eventually, you'll reap the rewards of your investments. In simple words, you can assure yourself that with high rated certainty, your savings will most likely generate 6% above inflation return. Over time, this will offer your family a decent pool to rely on for your long-term financial needs.

MR. DOC AND MR. BASHFUL

Well, these are not their real names, but they do a good job representing the typical "somewhat decent" investors. When I say "somewhat decent," that means they are not speculators *on drugs*. Most of us tend to speculate based on news or discussions at work or influenced by some kind of trend.

There is another realm of speculators where individuals start making decisions based on trends, graphs, or news, and unfortunately, they may make decent returns in the very early stages of their venturing with their new fling. In some very unfortunate situations, this money-making plays out for a little too long; in catastrophic situations, it may endure for a few years, which builds a strong conviction among winners. It is like making a decision to go all out, and in the very near future to go swimming naked in the ocean while the tide goes out. And then there are some fortunate ones, who only lose some decent savings in the early years in their investment journey.

THE STORY OF DOC – LEARNING WHAT AN EXCELLENT BUSINESS REALLY IS

To create long-term financial success and become a skilled investor, it's important to stick to the fundamentals rather than relying on trends, luck, and probability.

I once had a client who was a doctor and had a very successful medical practice and very a successful family. On top of this, he was not caught up in showing off and was more interested in living a simple life. It was easy to tell from his lifestyle that he shared many traits of a good investor. However, being successful in his own respective industry, he believed his success would translate to investments as well. That being said, he had his viewpoints on investments and would regularly question my expertise.

Through training and their day-to-day professional life, doctors like to collect a lot of information before they diagnose and write a prescription. In the same way that doctors use blood work results, Doc also makes most of his investment decisions based on numbers.

Being too busy at work and with families, Doc didn't have much time on hand to finish a thesis on a particular investment; in many cases, this process can take a few years. All of this inevitably leads an individual to make a late entry into the investment cycle. However, this does not stop them from believing in their intelligence. All their lives, people like Doc try to stay active in the market, instead of leaving investment decisions to experts.

After about three years of my managing his retirement accounts, we met one day at his office; Doc started the conversation by introducing a new company he had heard of from his pharmaceutical wholesaler. From experience I knew that this company would fall under one of three categories: a company chased by hot money, a company listed on a venture exchange that has to do with mining or technology, or a company that they deal with personally (i.e. if they are in some kind of auto industry, they will bring up names from the auto sector).

That particular day Doc brought up a company called CR Bard, a big player in heart stent, catheters, and medical devices. Doc's wholesaler heard of CR Bard from his brother-in-law, the Chief Financial Officer of a medical devices company in the States. His company was one of the companies bought out by CR Bard. This CFO happened to sit on the same table with the CEO of CR Bard and was highly impressed. Somehow this excitement moved on to Doc through the wholesaler.

It was early spring and the first hot day of the year. Doc showed no interest in my financial planning ideas or reviewing last year's performance. During most annual client meetings, the time was spent on discussing portfolio returns if numbers were negative; less time is needed to discuss them if portfolio numbers were positive. After Doc had shared some stories about his last trip to India, he jumped onto his new hope diamond CR Bard, a veteran of medical devices, and trading on NYSE. Lucky for me he gave little details on CR Bard's business and their leadership in Catheter, stents, and other surgical devices and followed with straight question – whether or not I knew about CR Bard.

This was my first time hearing that name, and of course, I had no clue about their business, but still my answer was yes. Tactfully, I said I knew the name but never did any research on them, since a client expects a professional financial advisor to know every public business. For me as a sales person, I could not answer no.

Without much delay, I took Warren Buffett's umbrella approach and warned Doc on the dangers of only investing in health care companies. I explained why diversification is mandatory for common investors like us. I almost won, as in those days it used to be very hurtful for my ego if a client won any discussion on either the markets or an individual stock, and had no shame making some predictions to prove I knew anything and everything about investing. I left Doc's office after promising I would do more work on CR Bard.

I went back and started researching the company. Within a few minutes, I came up with critical information proving two key points in support of my diversification belief. The first one was that from 1987 to 1989 CR Bard had faced fiery competition from Pfizer and Eli Lilly in their top market of coronary catheters. Second, in 1993 C.R. Bard was blamed for two deaths and had to pay over 60 million for misrepresentation of information on their angioplasty catheters, having to take angioplasty catheters out of the market.

20 minutes of research was all it took. Doc was impressed by my "in-depth knowledge" and was okay without me adding CR Bard to his portfolio. However, he kept track of the company's day-to-day stock price and rubbed it in many times over the next few years until the financial crisis happened. As Warren Buffett says, "only when the tide goes out, do you discover who's been swimming naked."

Point here being, Doc wanted to invest in the stock not because it was actually an excellent business, but rather because his business contact told him it was. Time and time again, it prevailed that an excellent business was decided based on business models and diversification and not because it appeared to be a shiny object.

BASHFUL – THE PRUDENT INVESTOR

I'm a firm believer that there are three types of people. The first type of person, excuse my language, is stupid. This person will make a mistake and not learn from it, ultimately making the same mistake over and over again. The second type of person is smart. A smart person will make a mistake and learn from it, ensuring he/she never makes the same mistake again. The third type of person is prudent. Someone who is prudent avoids making their own mistakes by simply learning from other people's mistakes. Bashful was the third kind of person: prudent.

Bashful was a highly educated hard-worker with very high integrity. Mr. Bashful joined the Indian Army after grade 12 and completed his MBA free of cost while simultaneously working for the Army. After much success in India, he retired early and moved to Canada at the age of 50. Bashful quickly found a job in an auto parts company that offered him decent wages, along with all the health benefits he needed. He used the accounting skills he learned during his MBA to supplement his income and started filing personal income tax returns. Soon enough, he had over 100 clients. On top of this, Bashful acted as their immigration and legal advisor. In the last few years of his practice, he made some good money by arranging mortgages and lines of credits for his income tax clients and their friends.

Within the first 10 minutes of our meeting, I told him my belief in buying affordable term (temporary) life insurance and investing the rest in retirement or education saving plans. It was around 1 pm, and I asked him if would like to join me for lunch. As I drove out of my parking lot with Bashful in the passenger seat, his phone rang. His client inquired whether he and his wife, as well as their children, should sign up for insurance policies that evening. Bashful's answer was a straightforward no, followed by a long lecture on how term insurance is a better choice.

Not only did he repeat everything I told him just a half an hour before, but he also added one more piece of advice – his son did not need any life insurance as no one is dependent on him financially. Instead, they should use those dollars for savings in a government sponsored education plan, since education is the best investment and insurance for his age. I was impressed.

Not only did Bashful learn from my mistakes that I had made years earlier, but he wholeheartedly listened to my experience and applied it, further helping his own clientele.

WHEN CAB MEDALLIONS WERE ALL THE RAGE

With a strict template on what an excellent business is and what it can offer, I've experienced many fads disguised as excellent businesses come and go, Taxi Cab Medallions were one of these fads.

In the mid - 2000's the rat race was all about medallion cab prices. Due to efforts from lobbyist groups, owning a cab plate worked out to be a pretty good investment for North American investors for many decades. A large proportion of cab drivers in the Greater Toronto Area were of Indian origin, and after almost two decades of renting, many drivers of Indian origin started buying medallions financed from secured lines of credit, often against their home. Fortunately, both rents and real estate prices started an upward journey from 1995 onwards, and because of high demand and low interest rates, medallion prices kept their pace alongside real estate valuations. The majority of drivers worked long hours (on average over 60 hours a week) and led simple lives, using almost all their savings plus most of their home equity to add to their medallion ownership. At one point around 2005, the average owner of a medallion owned approximately 1.5 medallions. Almost all of them had no retirement savings and were relying exclusively on their spouse's savings and rent expectations from their medallions as their future savings pot.

Most of my cab driving clients were in their 50's, and whenever I brought up the topic of retirement savings with them, they had an exact understanding of the revenue they expected to earn from medallion rent after retirement. These numbers were sufficient to maintain the lifestyle that they were accustomed to and with their numbers being correct, I had no choice but to keep my mouth shut. That being said, I strongly urged them to get rid of their mortgages and continue to advise them to sell part of their medallion ownership to achieve this important financial objective. This was in 2006, and unfortunately, only two took my advice.

For those that kept their medallions, this worked out to be the worst financial decision many of them made, for rent and housing prices continued to rise. One of my clients was so upset, he not only took his wife's retirement account to another advisor, he made sure to schedule an appointment in order to give me a good dose of verbal abuse. I always had a good pitch against the pricing of medallions, which had three dimensions:

1) If interest rates increased substantially
2) If the economy went into a recession
3) If the municipality decides to issue more medallions

If any of these three factors occurred, prices would go down significantly because all the value of medallions resided in goodwill. I was, again, very wrong on all these three fronts, and not one of these happened until 2015.

What happened was something no one had predicted, something that I had not even the faintest idea about during my attack on medallion pricing. The thing that happened — the thing no one could have predicted — is the darling of today's' riders, and a weapon of mass destruction for cab owners. Uber.

A staple characteristic of an excellent business is its ability to handle business risk. Does the business have a large enough competitive moat[2] to handle pressure from competitors? Does the business have diversified revenue streams to pick up the slack when one area isn't doing well? It's now clear that cab medallions didn't fulfill either aspect.

Sometimes, the best way to avoid getting caught up in your own success is by being prudent when learning from other peoples' mistakes. Using other people's brains is a good way to start.

---

[2] Competitive Moat: A term coined by Warren Buffett to determine how well a business can protect itself, and maintain revenues, in spite of competition.

CHAPTER VI:
USE OTHER PEOPLE'S BRAINS

"Know it for certain that without steady devotion for the Guru and unflinching patience and perseverance, nothing is to be achieved." – **Swami Vivekananda**

Hundreds of years ago in the Indus Valley of India, looking for and following a spiritual guru was almost genetically engraved in the people living in that geographical region. When I say guru, I use the word as a synonym for a teacher with no religious connotation.

The word guru comes from two syllables: one is "gu" meaning *darkness*, and other "ru," meaning *light*. Hence, your guru or teacher sheds the light of knowledge, which takes away fears of darkness from your life. This simple, but very powerful outcome from the teacher-student relationship is found in almost all worldly matters, such as literature, yoga, cooking, law, business, and financials. In this new Google era, you can find and follow a guru while sitting in the comfort of your living room. By learning from the mistakes of others and using other people's brains, not only can you take advantage of lucrative opportunities, but you can also refrain from making costly mistakes.

Similarly, when purchasing stocks or equities, it's easy to listen to your friends and use their brain. But why do that when you can listen to the experts instead? This is a lesson my friend Mr. Singh has learned the hard way.

THE STORY OF MR. SINGH – WHEN LISTENING TO THE EXPERTS GOES RIGHT

Mr. Singh was in his early 70s when I first met him. He migrated to Canada with barely a dollar to his name and being a diligent, relentless man he managed to establish a solid foundation for himself and his family in Canada. He worked extremely hard, committing himself to 12-hour rotating shifts five to six times a week on an automotive assembly line. Mr. Singh was frugal with his money, saving much of his earnings in his bank account. Unfortunately, he earned next to nothing in interest due to low bank interest rates at the time. He soon grew weary of simply saving his money; he wanted to find new profitable alternatives to grow his wealth.

As all good investors acknowledge, in order to make money you have to use the money, a methodology Mr. Singh adopted. He started buying and selling real estate in addition to buying and holding gold - both of these ventures provided steady returns. Even with his solid real estate and gold success, Mr. Singh was eager to continue growing his wealth.

Mr. Singh is a passionate golfer. Near the end of 1999, Mr. Singh was engaged in a conversation with fellow golfers who were bragging about their portfolio returns for the past year. They protruded their earnings substantially by investing in technology. This peaked Mr. Singh's interest; he was impelled to open a discount broker account of his own, using a few thousand dollars to start. Over the course of the next year, he continued to invest in stocks.

At the end of 2000, Mr. Singh encountered his golfing friends again. This time, he would share some success stories of his own. His success with technology stocks stemmed from a few set rules he strictly abided by, which he proclaimed "the do's and don'ts in trading technology stocks." Some of these rules were: (1) only buy Nasdaq listed, (2) avoid TSE listed stocks, (3) only buy stocks that are trading under five dollars, (4) put a stop order, etc. Unfortunately, these rules did not hold up well against the 2001 technology bust. Just like everybody else, Mr. Singh lost one-third of his life savings within two years of his new venture.

Mr. Singh possessed a tranquil demeanor, and he did not complain much about his unfortunate losses. Instead, he regrouped and carried on with his life. It was not until 2003 when gold prices were on the rise that Mr. Singh decided to give the stock market a second shot. His relative told him about a Canadian Gold Mining company worth investing in. With the rising gold prices on his mind, he gave it some consideration, immediately investing a large amount of money into that stock. In an odd turn of events, the gold stock sky rocketed in a very short amount of time, meaning Mr. Singh was back on top once again. This was when he came to me. We talked and drew similarities between Gold and the NASDAQ stocks he once owned. We agreed that as the tech stocks, Gold was widely speculative and rather than invest more, the smarter option would be to leave the party early. He wisely sold everything and recovered all of his losses from the technology bust. To say he was lucky is an understatement. Mr. Singh won the lottery that day.

With an open mind and the willingness to listen, Mr. Singh was very lucky in the end. In this case, a financial advisor helped him out. I believe the same can be true for you.

HOW TO FIND A GOOD FINANCIAL ADVISOR

When it comes to finding the right investment advisor or portfolio manager, it's important to look at both qualitative and quantitative factors. Failing to consider either of the two will result in subpar performance over the long-term.

In reality, managing money is more than just being smart. There is a strong emotional aspect to money management that is often overlooked. Having a strong intellectual framework will ensure that your manager makes the right decision, regardless of what the markets or the media are saying. And believe me, this is a lot harder than it sounds.

Unfortunately, there are not many experts, and if there are some, you can only meet them through books or websites. Since there are millions of pages of information on websites and books, the common investor stays confused and unable to follow one or a handful of gurus for life like investment trends. Both role models and gurus come and go with trends and short-term results.

Warren Buffet once said, "We simply attempt to be fearful when others are greedy and to be greedy only when others are fearful." With the herd-like mentality that many investors adopt, it's important to maintain a clear understanding of the inherent value of stocks that you own or may purchase. It's always best to look for strategic opportunities rather than opting for getting rich quick schemes or chasing shiny objects.

With that in mind, I've created a list that may be of use when selecting a money manager.

1. **Integrity.** You must be able to trust this person with your money and believe they will always do what's in your best interest.

2. **Honesty and transparency.** Will your money manager be truthful and open with their decisions? If a manager is unwilling to tell you why they are making the investment decisions, that is a problem!

3. **Proven track record and past performance.** This one is self-explanatory. Although past performance doesn't necessarily indicate future success, it does provide credibility. Choose a manager that has consistently beaten the market over the long-term.

4. **Ability to think rationally.** This is most important, in my opinion. The markets are **not** rational and often behave in mysterious ways. It's easy to get caught up in the hype when a stock is doing well or to be pessimistic when it is doing poorly. But investment decisions should be made on the fundamentals of business; in the long run, performance will take care of itself.

CHOOSE CERTAINTY OVER PROBABILITY

There is a realm of speculation where individuals begin making decisions based on trends, graphs, or news. Unfortunately, these individuals may make decent returns during the very early stages with their new fling. In some very unfortunate situations, this money-making plays out for a little too long; in catastrophic situations, it may endure for a few years, which builds a strong conviction among winners. One day, these winners will decide to go all in, and at some point in the very near future, go swimming naked in the ocean while the tide goes out. On the other hand, there are some fortunate ones who only lose some decent savings in the early years of their investment journey.

CHAPTER VII:
USE OTHER PEOPLE'S MONEY

"When you combine ignorance and leverage, you get some pretty interesting results." - **Warren Buffett**

It's very controversial, however very important principal in today's highly leveraged economies and households. Today, households of the richest country like Canada are carrying record high household debts. This simple phenomenon of using other people's money for your own needs very rapidly changing more towards wants than needs. We have just gone through the very painful experience in our neighbouring South where millions of households and hundreds of banks suffered losing all their savings in a matter of few months, and the one and only culprit of all this catastrophic human made tragedy was leveraging or in simple terms using too much of other people's money. Not getting into too many details of this very important principal let me help you with one technique, I call KISS - Keep It Simple, Sir. Use this principle only for appreciating assets like a mortgage for your principal home, education, or to set up your business. Avoid or decline using borrowed money for deprecating assets like cars, furnishings, vacations, and electronics.

Borrowing for investments is another trend building in the investment world. After 24 years of investment experience and all kinds of formal education, I'm not even that smart an investor to justify the risk associated with borrowing for investments. If you are reading this book and have come this far, I can conclude that you are also not fit to venture this and don't recommend it

CHAPTER VIII:
THE SKILLED INVESTOR VS. THE LUCKY GAMBLER

Throughout this book, we've been discussing ways to accumulate wealth for your family by acting like a skilled investor. But on the flip side, behaving like a lucky gambler and destroying your family's wealth is *much* easier! In fact, all it requires is three simple steps:

1. Use Leveraging
2. Be Greedy
3. Aim for Sky-High Returns

1. Use Leveraging

Leveraging: Borrowing Money

The first thing you need to do to destroy your family's wealth is leverage. Ensure you leverage efficiently by borrowing more than 100% of your family's net worth, and put this money towards investing in speculative assets such as options, futures, and foreign currency exchange.

All I want you to do is risk what you have and need for what you don't have and don't need. If you come across a quote from Warren Buffett, please don't read it.

Just in case you read his other saying, "I've seen more people fail because of liquor and leveraging - leverage being borrowed money. You really don't need leverage in the world much. If you are smart, you are going to make a lot of money without borrowing." Please ignore him and tell yourself that he is too old and that doesn't understand the modern financial world.

I don't even feel it's worth my time to mention that once this so called investment legend said "borrowed money is the most common way that smart guys go broke," so I won't.

2. Be greedy

When everyone is greedy, just follow the crowd and be greedy as well. Buffett says, "the fact that people will be full of greed, fear or folly is predictable. The sequence is not predictable."

I think you can predict them, if not ask your broker or sales person and please have faith in yourself and last but not least always rely on your luck.

3. Aim for Sky-high Returns

Don't even think about getting reasonable or good enough returns from your hard earned savings, instead, aim for sky-high returns. If your favorite investment has beat a broader index like the S&P 500 in the recent past, it can do the same or even better in the future.

So just ensure that your investment decisions are based on historical returns, especially returns from very recent past (last 5 years is good enough). Once this is done, you can start seeking high returns without wasting hours on doing valuations based on fundaments like the interaction of capital employed, the return on that capital, and future capital generated versus the purchase price.

Ignore anyone suggesting that the recent returns are the result of any bubble, with one strong conviction in your own belief that "things will be different this time."

In the modern capitalized world, not only is it very simple, but it is also very easy to destroy your family's hard earned wealth. For all of your decent investment returns during a boom time, many followers of Mr. Buffett will undermine your skills with sayings like, "In the short term, the highest returns often go to those who take the most risk." You know it is true for long-term returns also.

All you have to do is put your best efforts and train your mind to believe that all you are doing agrees with the right side column of the table from Nassim Taleb's book Fooled by Randomness. Let me warn you that your skilled investor friends will try to convince you that your recent results are because of left side actions.

Luck	Skill
Randomness	Determination
Probability	Certainty
Belief, conjecture	Knowledge, certitude
Theory	Reality
Anecdote, coincidence	Causality, law
Survivorship bias	Market outperformance
Lucky idiot	Skilled investor

If still, you wish to maintain your family's wealth, simply ignore everything I said above and do the opposite.

CHAPTER IX:
TRYING IT ALL TOGETHER – MY PARTING WORDS

Throughout this book, I've discussed ways you can grow your savings and investments while improving the state of your personal life at the same time. I hope you've gained clarity on where your finances are going, and why it's so much more important to pay attention to ways you can reduce your Interest, Insurance, and Income tax than to count pennies at your local coffee shop. With small changes like obtaining a part-time job, determining wants from needs, and so on, can certainly make an impact on your financial health, remember to analyze and criticize investment opportunities, such as those in real estate, before proceeding. There is no such thing as easy money, at least if you're interested in long-term security and financial protection.

The difference between the skilled investor and the lucky gambler is patience and perseverance. The skilled investor opts for certainty, depends on knowledge, pays attention to market outperformance, and looks at reality. The lucky gambler is random, relying on probability, conjecture, theory, and anecdotes. My goal is for you to become the former. You don't need to be a Portfolio Manager to develop a strong understanding of finance fundamentals. You can create a *wealthy* life for yourself by avoiding or minimizing debt, choosing well-considered opportunities, and making the most of your situation. While many prefer to play the lottery hoping to win the jackpot, you can produce your own opportunities simply by paying attention, doing your homework, and following the guidance in this book. It's perfectly natural to want to drive the nicest sports car, wear beautiful clothes, and to live in a big, impressive house. But speaking from experience and knowledge, living debt-free and developing close relationships with those who matter most is far more rewarding.

A humble mindset is all that's required. Surrendering to a guru's recipe and following it religiously is a much easier and arguably better way to learn and achieve your goals. During Buddha's time, seekers of any knowledge would spend years and years looking for the right guru. Though we continue to seek out gurus, we definitely cut this time short. The search is often limited to a few days or weeks. That said, modern minds have become a little arrogant and are often forced to learn the hard way — that is, they must make their share of mistakes before surrendering to a guru.

Money management is no different! Investing is one specific discipline in money management where this becomes evident. You can pull out all of the letters to shareholders by legends like Warren Buffett (Berkshire Hathaway) or Prem Watsa (Fairfax Holdings) and read and learn at your convenience. Again, the hard part involves surrendering your natural instincts like getting rich fast and persevering.

You might need to review several letters before grasping the essence of the investment style of these legends. Above all, it didn't cost you anything to learn, and you don't have to leave the comfort of your home. But by investing a few weeks of your valuable time, you will receive very simple, realistic, and practical knowledge on the subject of investing, and avoid wasting energy and money on costly and frustrating financial advisors working for big institutions. Before I conclude, I would like to recommend two books that I think will definitely help you in understanding the basics of investing (which is all you really need). The first one is *Learn to Earn* by Peter Lynch, and the second is *Intelligent Investor* by Benjamin Graham.

Throughout this book, I have introduced you to four modern investment Gurus: Warren Buffett, Prem Watsa, Peter Lynch, and Benjamin Graham. Depending on your passion or needs, you can get enough light from these to shed all the darkness in your investment world. In general, it's a widely believed phenomenon that to achieve success in any field all you need is to have some kind of role model who has achieved tremendous success. Look for their recipe and start cooking your own success without adding your own egoistic emotional ingredients.

ABOUT THE AUTHOR

Ravi's money management story started in 1992. As an immigrant to Canada with $5 in his pocket, he became a financial advisor at Berkshire Securities (now Manulife Securities) and was one of their top producers. Through his solo practice eventually managed investments for over 300 clients. After 21 years, he decided to start his firm, Sodhi Asset Management Inc. – SAMI Canada.

Today, he is a Portfolio Manager and the President at SAMI Canada. He has accumulated over 24 years of experience in the investment industry, advising and helping Canadian families to find peace and financial security for the future.

Ravi attributes his success to learning from legends including Warren Buffet, Charlie Munger, and Benjamin Graham. He cultured himself to prefer *Growth at a Reasonable Price* companies and believe that the best returns will come from high-growth companies that sell well below their intrinsic values. He is proud of his ethical reputation and spotless compliance record in which he always places his clients first and serves them with excellence.

Ravi has recently obtained his Global Professional Masters of Law from the University of Toronto. He is also a Fellow of the Canadian Securities Institute and holds the CFP and CIM designations.

Made in the USA
San Bernardino, CA
10 February 2017